Jesus as King in Education

A Simple Guide to Seeking the
Kingdom of God in Education

David Freeman

JESUS AS KING IN EDUCATION
© Copyright 2019 — David Freeman

All rights reserved. This book is protected under the copyright laws of the United Kingdom. No part of this publication may be reproduced, stored in a retrieval system or transmitted in any form or by any means, including electronic, mechanical, photocopying, recording or otherwise, without the prior written permission of the copyright owner, except by a reviewer, who may quote brief passages in a review.

This book may not be copied or reprinted for commercial gain or profit. The use of short quotations is permitted and encouraged.

Design by LifeVoiceQuest.com

ISBN : 978-1-9998755-2-7

For worldwide distribution. Printed in the United Kingdom.

Contents

About the Author

1 Jesus' Priority Commandment   7

2 The Kingdom of God in the Classroom   13

3 The Kingdom and Children: Our Pupils   21

4 The Word of God in Kingdom Education   31

5 Is the Kingdom in What We Teach?   37

6 Character Education   51

7 The Power of Children Praising the King's Presence   65

David Freeman

Independent Education Consultant
and Director of HighLight
www.highlightonline.org

David's career in education spans over 45 years. He trained and worked in the state system and then was invited to become the pioneering founding head of an independent all-age school near Oxford, England. The school has enjoyed an excellent reputation and consistently high academic results despite being non-selective. During his 17 years as Principal, David led a national team of educators in the UK for ten years.

David is Director of HighLight, which aims to 'unlock wisdom' in education and aims to inspire and equip educators, offering key principles to help them be effective in their teaching and mentoring. Over many years David has worked as an education consultant. He has an interest in helping developing countries. He has also helped to set up schools in Uganda, Rwanda, South Korea, Poland, and Kazakhstan. He is honorary principal of a school in S. Korea where he spent 3 months. In addition, he has helped to train teachers and leaders in Canada, the USA, Ghana, India, Norway, Holland and and presently mentors several leaders in education.

David is the author of the book 'Diamonds Lost in the Sand' which is about Christian education and 'The Knight-Charger', about the English education system. He is married to Rosie and they live in Henley-on-Thames, Oxfordshire. They have 3 children, now married, and 11 grandchildren.

Chapter One

JESUS' PRIORITY COMMANDMENT

In Matthew's gospel Jesus' priority commandment for all Christians is *'Seek first the kingdom of God and his righteousness' (Matthew 6:33)*. Jesus is making this a clear priority for our lives: to aim to search out the way to live, according to the King.

This commandment is not just for churches or individual Christians but for every aspect of life, including education. Jesus told the parable comparing the kingdom of God to yeast being mixed into bread dough. The yeast permeates every part of the bread mixture, changing it completely in size, shape and texture. This illustrates the fact that the kingdom of God, once we receive it, begins to challenge and change every part of our lives. God's plan is also for it to affect every area of society—including education—through Christians.

We are to make the kingdom of God our first priority and aim to live rightly related to God, which is the meaning of seeking his 'righteousness.' Jesus tells teachers and school leaders to seek the kingdom first and all these other things you need: truth, revelation, knowledge, wisdom, finance, help, patience, ability, strength (and more) will be added to you.

This booklet is asking: 'What does the kingdom of God look like in education?

What does it look like in a school? What does it look like in the classroom? Before we can explore and try to answer these questions, we need to try to define the kingdom of God.

How May We Define the Kingdom of God?

The kingdom of God is both present and future — both here and not yet fully here. American theologian George E. Ladd wrote a book on the kingdom of God called 'The Presence of the Future'. This aptly combines the two facets of the kingdom. Jesus, during his ministry on earth, explained that the kingdom of God was present in him and demonstrated through what he did. At the start of his 3-year ministry he declared, "Repent for the Kingdom of heaven is near."[1] *'Kingdom of heaven'* and *'Kingdom of God'* are interchangeable terms meaning the same thing in scripture. As he demonstrated Father's love and power through healings and deliverance he stated, "But if I drive out demons by the Spirit of God, then the kingdom of God has come upon you."[2]

The Kingdom was present in him and through these works but it was not fully on earth — this would await the preaching of the gospel to all nations and only on his final return to judge the earth will the kingdom of God be fully established in a new heaven and earth. Only in the last days of earth does the angel in the book of Revelation sound the seventh trumpet and it is declared, *'The kingdom of the world has become the kingdom of our Lord and of his Christ, and he will reign for ever and ever.'*[3]

---

1 Matthew 3:2

2 Matthew 12:28

3 Revelation 11:15

Here and Still to Come

The kingdom of God is both presently here, and it is also growing amongst us until the final end times. For born-again Christians living on earth since Christ's resurrection, the kingdom is present, (even though not fully so) through the rule of King Jesus in our hearts and the choices in which we follow his directions.

I was involved in helping to set up a new Christian school in 1984. In those early days we were learning about the kingdom of God but we did not really know how to be a 'Christian' school. However, we wanted to 'seek first the kingdom of God in education' so we asked about everything, "Jesus, how should we do this?' This included daily structure, devotions, assemblies, reports, parents' evenings as well as our teaching and our discipline. How were we to be different for God's purposes?"

As Jesus and the Father are one, a simple definition of the kingdom of God is: 'Father's will done in Father's way'.

A fuller definition by an experienced educator:

'The kingdom of God is the sphere of God's active rulership in people's hearts by the Father through the Son, Jesus Christ, in the power and presence of the Holy Spirit.'[4]

---

4 Dr. Dow Robinson

So Where Is It?

Jesus said 'The kingdom of God is within you'.[5] It is true that if we have accepted Jesus as Saviour and King, he is within us as he promised.

'If anyone loves me, he will obey my teaching. My Father will love him and we will come to him and make our home with him.'[6]

Another way of saying that the kingdom is within you is to say that it is among you, corporately. The word 'you' is plural; and there is meant to be a corporate expression of the kingdom through Christ's body on earth.

In any sphere of life, the kingdom is not an institution but it is manifest through Christians. The kingdom of God cannot be fully in education unless it comes through his servants: the teachers and leaders. This means that we must aim for the school to be an extended family rather than an institution.

---

5 Luke 17:21

6 John 14:23

Chapter Two

THE KINGDOM OF GOD IN THE CLASSROOM

How do we know if our classroom is expressing the kingdom of God? What are the signs of the kingdom of God in the teachers and in the classroom?'

One educator expressed it this way, 'The classroom is a small community in which we daily practise living in the kingdom of God.'

The Role of the Teacher

The role of the teacher is vital in the education process: they set the atmosphere. Any teacher can advance or hinder the Kingdom in the classroom. A caring teacher who operates with grace and patience will build the essential bridge of relationship needed for the conveying of knowledge, understanding and wisdom. Jesus as Rabbi (teacher) to his disciples is our model.

Conversely, an impatient, unfeeling or easily angered teacher will have a detrimental effect on the pupils. The atmosphere created by such a teacher is one of tension pressure and even fear. By contrast, the teacher operating in peace and well-being sets an atmosphere of peace and joy conducive to learning. This teacher affirms and encourages his or her pupils and, over the positive bridge of relationship learning can be received by the pupil. In this atmosphere pupils flourish and are more likely to become disciples of the teacher. I believe God meant education to be imparted from the living to the living with expressive life!

Whilst pupils are often forgetful, the caring and supportive teacher is remembered by pupils with affection for many years. The Times Educational Supplement magazine in England carries regular testimonies of famous celebrities in sport and the media who were envisioned and encouraged in their gifting by a discerning, caring teacher. A teacher who 'loves' (unconditionally accepts) their pupils will still need to bring correction and discipline for their children. But it will be redemptive even when punishing. (More of this later in this chapter.) The kingdom teacher sets sensible boundaries for behaviour which enhance the classroom's kingdom community. These will give security and ultimately bring peace, even when opposed initially by the pupils. For more on this see 'The Role of the Teacher' available by request from HighLight.[1]

The Sign of LOVE

The first and major sign must be love because God the King is love[2] and the kingdom demonstrates the love of God.

Love sets an atmosphere in the school. However, as love is such an overused word, we need to unpack it to get the meaning that God intended. In the

---

1 A Key document: 'Teacher as Role Model' available by request by email to office@highlightonline.org See also www.highlightonline.org for more about HighLight.

2 1 John 4:16

English language it is a very overworked word: I love my wife; I love my dog; I love McDonalds!

The Greek word used for God's love is *agape* which means a one-way love that is given regardless of whether or not it is returned. This is how Jesus loved us even while we were still his enemies.

In his excellent book on the kingdom of God, Edward Carnell wrote, 'Whoever would enter the Kingdom of God must first enter the kingdom of love'.[3] He defines love in the following way:

"Love is an act of unconditional acceptance. It receives another person just as he is, without one plea. It raises no legal barriers.; it says, 'I accept you; you count.' Love is always kind and truthful, and seeks nothing but kindness in return."[4]

Jesus expressed it in what is often called his 'golden rule'. "Do to others as you would have them do to you"[5] or put another way: 'Treat one another the way you would like to be treated.'

Not only must the teacher unconditionally accept each pupil and give them respect, regardless of their academic ability, but they also have to be taught how to accept and value each other, despite many differences of personality and gifting.

---

3 Carnell, J. *The Kingdom of God and the Pride of Life*, p23

4 Carnell, J. *The Kingdom of God and the Pride of Life*, p7

5 Luke 6:31

Love Is Also Correction

In addition, real love means there will be correction for wrong attitudes and wrong behaviour.[6] The whole area of setting and implementing boundaries for the right behaviour in a class is of great importance but is beyond the scope of this guide.[7] However, it is important to say that the right, just and fair boundaries will enhance the peace of the kingdom in your class or school. All discipline/correction needs to be redemptive and should lead to a transformation of character.

The Sign of THE WORD OF GOD

One of Jesus' titles is 'The Word of God'. This means he is the expression of God: he speaks as God and reveals God's nature and ways and this produces a worldview. The Word of God is vital for our pupils to read, to know, to meditate upon and to memorise. It must be at the centre of character development, and central to our curriculum. Through our devotions, and the curriculum we use, we are teaching our pupils a worldview;[8] which means how we live and view the world from Father God's perspective. Even where we are required to teach a government curriculum, we can insert the perspective of the word of God. We call this a heart concept or truth at the heart of the lesson and is one

---

[6] *Behaviour Management, HighLight Key document. All Key documents mentioned are available on request. Visit www.highlightline.org..*

[7] *Diamonds Lost in the Sand by the author, deals more fully with this topic (available on Amazon)*

[8] *HighLight's Worldview Key explains this further*

way we teach how to ensure our teaching is God-centred.[9] This is more fully expanded in Chapter 5.

Other Signs of the Kingdom in the Classroom

The apostle Paul expressed the kingdom in this way: *'The kingdom of God is righteousness, peace and joy in the Holy Spirit.'*[10]

The key word here is 'in'. The kingdom is only present in the Spirit of God and wherever he is welcomed. He is in every born-again Christian teacher but we will need the help of the Holy Spirit in everything if the kingdom of God is to be made manifest in the atmosphere. We all know how quickly atmosphere can change and peace be lost by sinful behaviour in the classroom!

The Sign of RIGHTEOUSNESS

This is to do with being and doing what is right by God's standards and being in right relationship with him. Righteousness means:

- Respecting God with worship
- Respecting God's word
- Right teacher-pupil and pupil-to-pupil relationship
- Reconciliation and forgiveness after disputes and quarrels

---

9 HighLight offers training sessions or individual mentoring on how to develop Christian curriculum: called 'The Way to Wisdom'

10 Romans 14:17

- Respect for authority
- Respect for one another as made in God's image
- Faithfulness by the teacher in planning, marking and making right assessments of work
- Pupils being honest in tests and not copying wrongly

The Sign of PEACE

- Peace is the result of just and fair government by the teacher.
- Peace also results from good order in the classroom. 'God is not a God of disorder or confusion but of peace.'[11] The good teacher will plan an orderly routine and classroom.
- Peace results when pupils are treated fairly and their work loads are right for their ability.

The Sign of JOY

Jesus had more joy than all those around him. Why was this? Because, Psalm 45 says prophetically about him, *'You love righteousness and hate wickedness; therefore God, your God, has set you above your companions by anointing you with the oil of joy.'*

Joy is found in:

- Doing what is right. Do right and you will feel right!

---

11 Paraphrased from 1 Corinthians 14:33

- A happy teacher: we are the 'book' the pupils read[12]
- Praising and worshipping God
- Pleasing the teacher and doing the right thing
- Giving to one another
- Teamwork
- Sharing good news
- Celebrating success

Keep seeking FIRST the active rule and will of Christ the King in these ways, depending on the Holy Spirit through prayer, and the kingdom of God will steadily increase around you!

---

12 2 Corinthians 3:2-6

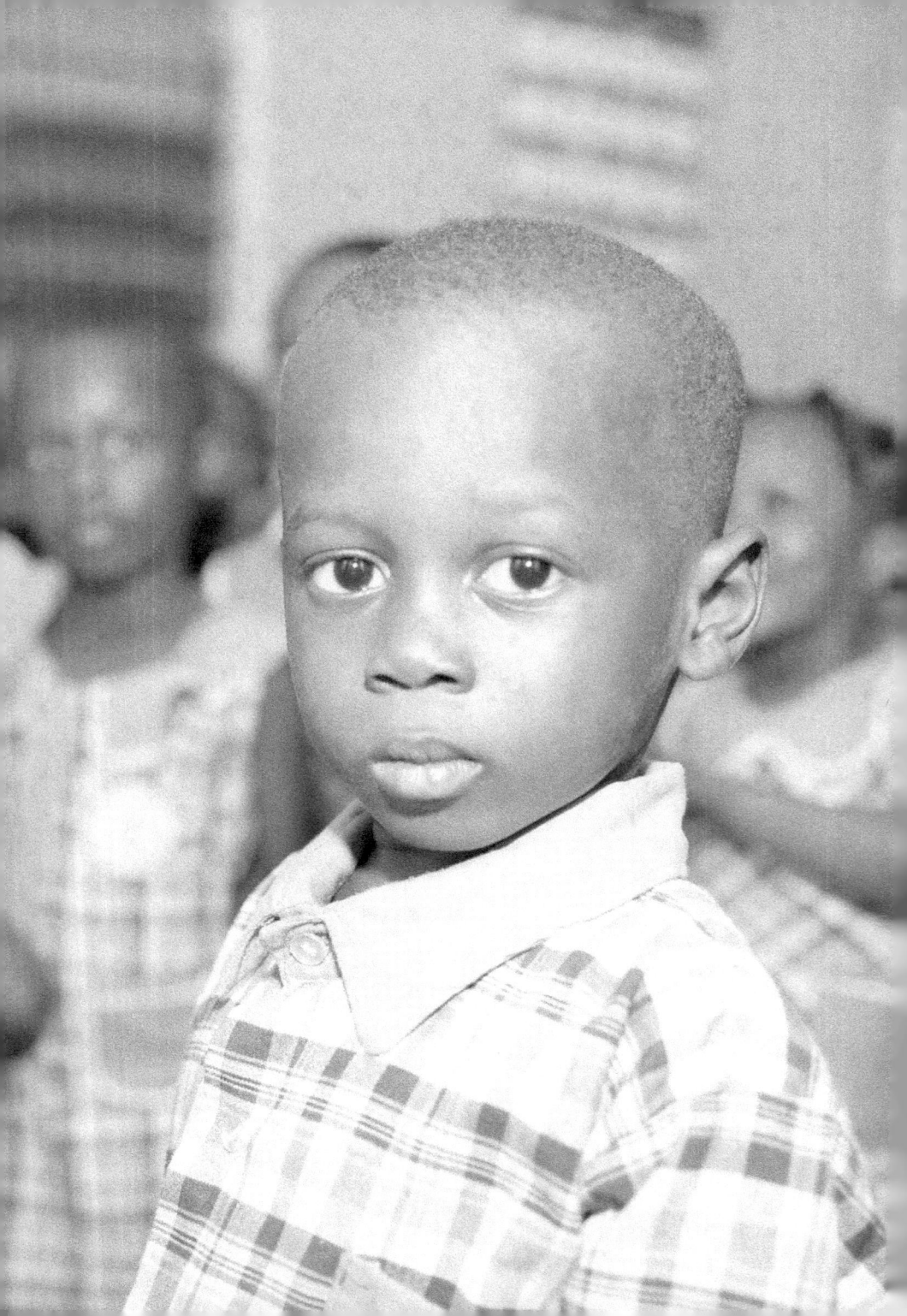

Chapter 3

THE KINGDOM AND CHILDREN: OUR PUPILS

In this chapter we explore the kingdom of God as it relates to children. On one occasion when mothers were bringing their children to Jesus, the disciples began to block them, no doubt regarding children as less important than adults. Jesus rebuked them and made a remarkable statement: *"Let the little children come to me, and do not hinder them, for the kingdom of heaven belongs to such as these."*[1] He then proceeded to value them by placing his hands on them and blessing them.

The kingdom perspective of God frequently needs to challenge our adult presumptions. In fact, Jesus said, *"Unless you change and become like little children you will never enter the kingdom of heaven."*[2] I remember when we had not long opened our school and I was a teaching head, I suddenly experienced the presence of God as I circulated to check on the children's work. It was sobering. I felt as though the Holy Spirit was at my shoulder and warning me: 'Be careful how you treat these children; they are God's creation'. I wish

---

1 Matthew 19:14

2 Matthew 18:4

I could say I always managed to be that aware of this truth but I can say it changed my perspective and, as an experience, it never totally left me and is still vivid many years afterwards.

God's word tells us that we are all, including every child, created in God's image in some way and that when we welcome a child, we are welcoming Jesus himself![3]

God is very protective of children and their faith. Amongst the many statements in Matthew's gospel chapter 18 he gives a most solemn warning:

'But if anyone causes one of these little ones who believe in me to sin, it would be better for him to have a large millstone hung around his neck and be drowned in the depths of the sea.'[4]

This is an awesome warning.

Unique Creations with a Unique Plan

Every child is a unique creation as seen in King David's Psalm 139, where he addresses God saying: *'For you created my inmost being; you knit me together in my mother's womb. I praise you because I am fearfully and wonderfully made ... All the days ordained for me were written in your book before one of them came to be.' (v13, 16)*

---

3 Matthew 18:5

4 Matthew 18:6

God has a plan for every life. Whether or not that plan is discovered depends on many factors, including the response of the individual to God. Jeremiah was spoken to by God in an amazing way when he was called, while only little more than a boy, to be a prophet of God. His calling gives us some very special insights, which I believe apply to every one of us.

'The word of the Lord came to me, saying, "Before I formed you in the womb, I knew you; before you were born I set you apart; I appointed you as a prophet to the nations."'[5]

This amazing statement reveals several precious things for us all as those made in God's image. First, God has formed us in the womb; but not only that, he says 'I knew you'. The word does not mean a casual knowing but an intimate knowing. This tells us that before conception God intimately knew Jeremiah—and, I believe, all of us. He chose to make us, each one. It also tells us that God had a plan and a purpose for Jeremiah's life—he was to be a prophet to the people of his time in Israel, sharing God's heart and challenges to them. It was a difficult task but God promised: 'I will be with you and I will rescue you.' This is true, for each one of us is created, as the apostle Paul tells us in his letter to the Ephesian church, *'For we are God's workmanship, created In Christ Jesus to do good works, which God prepared in advance for us to do.'*[6]

---

[5] Jeremiah 1:5
[6] Ephesians 2:10

Every One of Our Children Is Gifted!

Just as every child is a miracle creation, so God gives us gifts in order that we may fulfil our purpose in life. We need to recognise the varied nature of giftedness in our children. By 'giftedness' I mean the special talents or abilities that seem to be partly innate through heredity and partly learned. We hope this helps you to see your own children but also to consider the pupils you teach. The gifts they have may not fit our academic 'box'

This true story is told by a teacher:

'I have had three children and it has always amazed me that, although they are born from the same two parents, they are so very different in personality, in abilities and in gifting. My son is a pioneer, rather like me. He is a passionate speaker, artistic and very musical, writing his own worship songs and with his lovely wife has made a lovely worship CD. He is sporty and loves the outdoors. My two daughters are each different. One is organised and yet very artistic, a fairly private person, producing beautiful and sensitive paintings, yet she is not particularly musical but loves history. She also loves animals, especially dogs but likes her own company. My other daughter is very musical with a lovely voice, yet not artistic but a great home-maker; able to solve technical problems (which I can't!) but not a lover of animals. She has great compassion and is a carer of people.'

Every Child a Unique Child

God has created every one of our children uniquely. He has used our parental genes but yet he has crafted them and equipped them, each for a unique purpose and a plan in their lives.

Prior to the Fall, God's original plan was not for anything he made to be sub-standard. I believe every child is gifted no matter what their physical or mental condition. However, we may not recognise their gifts and calling if we have our own blinkered ideas of what 'gifted' really means. For some parents and teachers 'gifted' means only gifted in academic terms. Some children are created to think 'outside the box' and do not fit into our narrow categories. God will use them to do entrepreneurial or creative, imaginative pioneering.

Bear Grylls comes to mind as a person God has created to be kinaesthetically motivated (i.e. physically able and active) rather than academically or cognitively focused. Edward Michael 'Bear' Grylls is a British adventurer, writer and television presenter who specialises in daring outdoor challenges. Yet he uses his cognitive awareness in the outdoors to great advantage, enabling many to learn the arts of survival. However, there wasn't a 'survival' exam course in school to cater for him! We all know many students who are kinaesthetically motivated and gifted but have struggled with the confines of curricular subjects until they have been released to their chosen profession, often in athletics, sports, acting or outdoor pursuits. Yet they were specifically created by God for this. Samson is one biblical example of such a kinaesthetic man.

A Variety of Gifts

The Bible mentions a selection of different gifts in the book of Romans chapter 12 vv.4-8 and Ephesians 4:11-12. In Romans, Paul writes: *'We have different gifts, according to the grace given us.'*[7] The following gifts are mentioned:

---

7 Romans 12:6

Serving, prophesying, teaching, encouraging, governing in leadership and mercy or compassion.

In Ephesians several functional roles are listed. Some are created by God to be apostles in the church, some to be prophets, some to be evangelists and some to be pastors or teachers.

Now you may not be sure about the word 'apostle'. It was a Greek term used by the Romans. When conquering a territory, the Romans sent a man ahead to control the culture and to make it like Rome. Jesus used it and, in biblical terms, it means one 'sent' to get a job done, like the twelve apostles, or the apostle Paul. This gift is apparent today in those who are called by God to oversee a project and can designate the right people to the right tasks. They have a special gift of wisdom and relational ability to motivate others.

Are Practical or Artistic Skills Less Important than Academics?

There are many more gifts than are listed in those bible passages and we see them outworked in the practical craftwork gift of Bezalel and his helper, Oholiab, in Exodus 31. These two men were filled with the Spirit and gifted by God *'with skill, ability and knowledge of all kinds of crafts — to make artistic designs for work in gold, silver and bronze, to cut and set stones, to work in wood, and to engage in all kinds of craftsmanship.'*[8] Wow! What a gift for an important task! Be careful not to despise your child who is gifted with their hands at making things. They may be called by God to make something amazing for his glory one day!

---

8 Exodus 31: 2-6

Teachers need to learn to look at their pupils in this way. It is fun to try and spot the potential gifts in your children, even though they may as yet not be fully developed gifts as they are immature. Note that your child may have a combination of gifts!

In the following, see if you can spot the gifts from these clues that may be seen in immature children.

1. Humble, always offering to help, practical.
2. Generous, may give belongings away too easily.
3. Always ready to praise others, to get alongside those needing help.
4. Usually wants to be first, may be bossy, a challenger, looks ahead and sees the issues; other children follow.
5. Soft-hearted, gentle, aware of those hurting, may be over-sensitive.
6. Daring, pioneering, may be cheeky, has a bigger perspective.
7. Attractive to other children, popular, often a kind face, has many friends.
8. Articulate, good at explaining things, sense of order, a 1-2-3 steps person, may be bossy.
9. Easy-going, winsome, wants to be 'out there', finds it difficult to concentrate indoors or on detail.
10. Orderly, likes routine, sequential, tidy, organised, can be easily 'put out' by change.
11. Shrewd, can be critical and fault-finding.
12. Speaks out dramatically, often using colourful images, sometimes impulsively.

(Answers on the following chart)

Finally, some of our children suffer from disability or inherit our weaknesses; for example, dyslexic confusion over letters or numbers. I recommend an excellent book by Diana Hudson on specific learning difficulties.[9] Others may experience some form of damage or emotional 'bruising' in the birth process, or in relationships, or be traumatised by events or accidents. God has compassion on the weak and disadvantaged. Our Father has special love for them: *'A bruised reed he will not break, and a smouldering wick he will not snuff out.'*[10] Jesus, likewise, spoke of himself as gentle: *'Take my yoke upon you and learn from me, for I am gentle and humble in heart, and you will find rest for your souls. For my yoke is easy and my burden is light.'*[11]

---

9 Diana Hudson: *Supporting Specific Learning Difficulties: What Teachers Need to Know* available on Amazon and Kindle

10 Isaiah 42:3

11 Matthew 11:28-30

Some Biblical Gifts

1.	Humble, always offering to help, practical	Serving, helps
2.	Generous, may give belongings away too easily	Giver
3.	Always ready to praise others, to get alongside those needing help	Encourager
4.	Usually wants to be first, may be bossy, a challenger, looks ahead and sees the issues, other children follow	Leader
5.	Soft-hearted, gentle, aware of those hurting, may be over-sensitive	Mercy or compassion
6.	Daring, pioneering, may be cheeky, has a bigger perspective	May be apostolic
7.	Attractive to other children, popular, often a kind face, has many friends	Pastoral
8.	Articulate, good at explaining things, sense of order, a 1-2-3 steps person may be bossy	Teacher
9.	Easy-going, winsome, wants to be 'out there', finds it difficult to concentrate indoors or on detail	Evangelist
10.	Orderly, likes routine, sequential, tidy, organised, can be easily 'put out' by change	Administrator
11.	Shrewd, can be critical and fault-finding	Discernment
12.	Speaks out dramatically, using images, sometimes too impulsively	Prophetic

Chapter Four

THE WORD OF GOD IN KINGDOM EDUCATION

'Heaven and earth will pass away but my words will never pass away' (Matt.24:35)

Given this statement by Jesus Christ, how much are we, as schools with a Christian ethos, reflecting the importance of teaching the Word of God as integral to the education process?

An enormously powerful component in teaching, perhaps alongside the role model of the teacher, is the Word of God. Without a working knowledge of the Word of God our pupils will not be truly educated.

We have to understand that it is unlike any other word, for the Word of God contains power and is uniquely powerful in itself.

1. Power — it is living and active and has 'dunamis' (meaning strength, power or ability. It is the root of our English word 'dynamite'!)

'For the word of God is alive and active. Sharper than any double-edged sword, it penetrates even to dividing soul and spirit, joints and marrow; it

judges the thoughts and attitudes of the heart' (Hebrews 4:12).

2. Active—The Word of God contains power to activate. Once sown, like the seed Jesus spoke of in his parable, it contains life and is an ongoing 'doing' thing to fulfil the purpose for which it was sent. Isaiah prophesied that God's word *'will not return to me empty but will accomplish what I desire and achieve the purpose for which I sent it' (Isaiah 55:11).*

As Christian schools we need to honour, use, teach and love the Word of God; not as a heavy duty but as a joy, and use it as imaginatively as we can.

When pupils practise meditating on it, a love for more of the Word of God will grow, as long as this is not made a heavy activity. Psalm 19 gives us the following advantages of the Word of God:

- It refreshes you: it is perfect, reviving the soul
- It gives you wisdom: it can be trusted, making wise the simple
- It is true and right: it teaches what is right, giving joy to the heart
- It lights our way: it is radiant, giving light to the eyes
- It is pure: it teaches us the only good fear – respecting God
- It is dependable: it is sure and right

Historically, the Bible has shaped the foundations of our society and culture. 'The Bible was the keystone in the bridge to democracy.'[1] Whatever remains

---

1 Bragg, Melvin: The Book of Books, p335

of a humane, generally law-abiding and compassionate society, is largely due to the influence of the Word of God which, up until the 1960s, was an integral part of our national education system.

The Devotional Word

We have a pastoral role of teaching the Word of God in devotions in school. Whilst we recognise that it should be a parental joy and responsibility to share the Bible with our children, yet we need to recognise that many parents do not manage to find time to read or share it with their children — for all sorts of reasons. All the more important that we, as Christian schools, are giving time to explore its riches devotionally and in biblical studies. Such study leaves a rich deposit in our pupils' lives. One of the leavers from a Christian school testified how the memory verse learned many years earlier came to mind to provide a wise answer in a job interview! The Holy Spirit is faithful to remind us of truth.

The Word Is Foundational to Worldview

The Word of God in shaping worldview, ethics and moral values, is necessary for training disciples who choose to obey the Word and become men and women of integrity.

Worldview, the 'glasses' through which we understand the world, answers the big questions such as: "Why are we here?"; "What is the purpose of life?"; "What happens after we die?"; "Why is so much of the world in such trouble — what is wrong?" All these answers, and more, are found in the Bible. Our pupils need the opportunity to debate the ethical and moral questions and to learn what God's word says about these issues. This is a vital process for them in maturing in their points of view. The words of Jesus frequently challenge worldly thinking and personal motivation.

The Word of God Integrated in the Curriculum

It needs to be studied separately in Religious Education or other Biblical studies but God's word is relevant to all subjects and it should never be the intention that the Word of God be divorced from the curriculum, or from every subject in the curriculum. Christian teachers need to realise they are meant to be on a journey of revelation to appreciate the principles hidden in the Word of God for every subject and every aspect of knowledge, for it all belongs to God.

'In Him, (Jesus Christ) are hidden ALL the treasures of wisdom and knowledge.'[2]

This is a very important verse because it shows us that all knowledge and all wisdom is found in the person of Jesus Christ. He is the personification of all knowledge for use in education and much more besides. St Augustine famously said, *'All good Christians should understand that truth, wherever they may find it, belongs to their Lord.'*[3]

Not only is all knowledge in Jesus but all wisdom is too. This verse challenges us as educators. In the next chapter we will explore this further as the Word used in curriculum. The Word of God should not be verses 'bolted on'

---

2 Colossians 2:3

3 St Augustine. De Doctrina Christiana, II, 28

artificially to lessons. Rather, biblical principles need to be shown to be relevant to all aspects of learning.

The Word Is Jesus and Jesus Is the Word

The Word is the expression of God. Finally, in days when 'truth' is denied, argued over, and often rejected as an impossibility, the Word of God is truth. It is the expression of God. Jesus, as God, was not afraid to declare he is 'the Truth',[4] i.e. the true expression of his Father's word. In addition, Jesus was described by the apostle John as 'the Word of God'.[5] In the beginning was the Word and the statement of Jesus in Matthew's gospel[6] tells us that the Word of God will never pass away.

Let us be faithful stewards of its precious truth. The great reformer, Martin Luther said: "I am afraid that the schools will prove the very gates of hell, unless they diligently labor in explaining the Holy Scriptures and engraving them in the heart of the youth." Our schools are not institutions but family communities. Luther's statement warns us that, if our schools are to stay on course in demonstrating the kingdom of God; if they are to remain wholesome places; if they are to maintain their revelation and their cutting edge, the study of the Word of God is essential.

---

4 John's gospel 14:6
5 John's gospel 1:1
6 Matthew 24:35

Chapter Five

IS THE KINGDOM IN WHAT WE TEACH?

If all knowledge is in Christ, then this has got to affect our choice of curriculum. The kingdom is about righteousness so, whilst we cannot be too purist, we have to be aware of the content of textbooks or internet and online material we may use. Young children need protecting from stories of witchcraft and other evil. In fact, some of the traditional fairy stories are really frightening and not all suitable for young children as they can introduce fear. We need to ask ourselves: What is the message from this story? Is it wholesome? Is good triumphing over evil? Or is it promoting negative character issues? In addition, one of the foundational concepts to be taught and underlined in different ways is Creation and the image of God as our Creator. Therefore, we need to decide how to handle the curriculum material which automatically promotes evolution rather than creation. We have to decide in advance how we are going to handle these issues.

Knowledge in the World

In Genesis Satan successfully perverted this purpose of knowledge, ultimately hijacking God's plan for humankind until Jesus, the second Adam won it back. Satan caused Eve to desire this knowledge and 'wisdom' for selfish purposes. The consequence of this sin reverberates down through the ages and is currently expressed in secular humanism. As Satan originally suggested deceitfully and dishonestly to Eve, she could be wiser than God by her own volition, rather than being relationally dependent on God.

This is our temptation even to this present day. Knowledge is now mostly reduced to cerebral and cognitive knowledge by use of the mind's rational and logical processes, rather than including revelation out of a dependent relationship with God. Rational and logical processes are indeed part of God's purpose for man's mind. However, these processes need to be submitted to the Spirit of God. When knowledge becomes purely cerebral, it becomes self-centred and is used by man to promote himself and, with it, to gain power and control over others. Man then becomes 'always learning, but never able to come to the knowledge of the truth.'[1]

Wisdom Is Our Aim

In turn, wisdom is also reduced and limited to the application of man's intellectual knowledge and experience. Whilst this can be an aspect of wisdom, the true essence of wisdom is found in living our lives in relational obedience to God and being led by the Holy Spirit, who is the Spirit of wisdom. Wisdom is not, as the Greek inheritance leads us to believes, purely cerebral or intellectual. This panders to man's pride. In biblical terms wisdom is to do with how one we use our knowledge and apply it to make choices. Biblical wisdom means we make choices to please God. Jesus is our prime example, as he lived his life to please his Father. Therefore wisdom, not just knowledge,

---

1   2 Timothy 3:7

needs to be our aim for our pupils. Daniel in the Old Testament is also a fine example of wisdom through the choices he made in an alien and cruel society when he was enslaved.

Von Rad in his exploration of the complexity of Israel's wisdom says that for the Hebrew, '... the fear of Yahweh was the unutterable presupposition of knowledge. Inevitably, in a postmodern society that largely denies God, this has largely been lost in the learning that takes place in the world's universities today.'[2] By fear, he means reverence and humility which are the prerequisites of wisdom: *'When pride comes, then comes disgrace, but with humility comes wisdom.'*[3]

All Knowledge Belongs to God

The Spirit of God reveals to us the truth that every part of knowledge is related to God. As noted earlier, St. Augustine famously said: "Wherever truth be found let it declare that it belongs to its master." The Apostle Paul's revelation stated succinctly and bears repeating: *'In Him (Jesus Christ) are hidden all the treasures of wisdom and knowledge.'*[4] This short sentence is a tremendous statement with huge implications for education. If ALL, not some(!), of the treasures of wisdom and knowledge are hidden in Jesus Christ, then there is no knowledge or wisdom outside of him! Let us explore how this can be revealed in curriculum and how it will lead to the wisdom God wants to impart to us and our children.

---

2   Gerhard Von Rad: The Wisdom of Israel, p295

3   Proverbs 11:2

4   Colossians 2:3

In education knowledge is the battlefield. These two diagrams illustrate the difference between humanistic knowledge which makes man central to all knowledge. By contrast, the second diagram illustrates knowledge which places God at the centre and aims to reveal God in every curriculum subject.

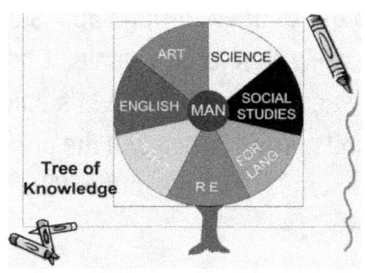 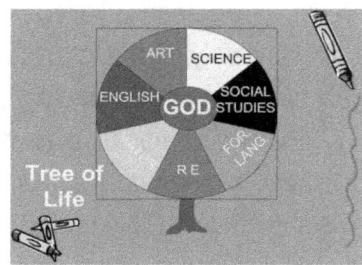

Every Subject Relates to God and His Wisdom

From a kingdom perspective, every subject represents an aspect of the knowledge of God and his world that he wants us to experience in order to lead us to greater wisdom. Every subject relates to him and is a facet of his wonderful character. God is a mathematician, a linguist, a scientist, an artist, a musician, a geographer and so on.

Chapter 1 of Genesis introduces us to all subjects of the curriculum in an embryonic way. In this account of creation there is language, mathematical order, astronomy, science, geography, history, anthropology and many more. The subjects are all integrated into the one whole creation story. In curriculum we need to remember that subjects belong to God and that they can be wonderfully integrated even while we still need to study them separately in depth. There is much art in science, maths and history and geography; there is much maths in physics chemistry, as well as in music. There is geography in history and history in science etc! In the following, clues of God can be seen in all subjects

Mathematics

Mathematics is based on the reason, order and logic with which God created his universe. In his fascinating book, James Nickel[5] explores the history of mathematics and the effect of religion and philosophy upon it. He says: "Mathematics is 1) but a tool, a servant that 2) aids man in unravelling the wisdom of God found in the harmonies and wonders of his works."[6] Is God a mathematician? Most definitely! If he is God of creation then number was created by him and reflects his nature through its order and his eternal essence is reflected through its infinity. There is no highest number; you can always add another one! Mathematics is challenging for the majority of children because it requires systematic logic. It also requires obedience: in order to get the answer to any problem or calculation you must follow the correct steps. How frustrated I used to become by those long multiplication or division sums where one small numerical error could make the whole answer wrong! We had no calculators when I was at school! We need patient teachers who can impart faith in the learning process!

Addition and multiplication reflect his increase; subtraction his decrease. Division represents justice and equity. Fractions represent the fact that in God's world everything, including us, is meant to be part of something larger and

---

5   J. Nickel: *Mathematics: Is God Silent?*
6   J. Nickel: *Mathematics: Is God Silent?* p43

everything can be dissected into smaller parts. We are at once a whole person but also a fraction of a larger gathering such as our family, our class, our community or our country. "You are all Christ's body and each one is a part of it."[7] This scripture describes us as both a whole number and a fraction. There are many accounts of measurement and calculation in the Bible (Noah's ark, the Temple) and, of course, there is even a book dedicated to Numbers!

Science

The word Science is derived from the Latin *scientia* which simply means knowledge. It has come to be applied to a specific area of knowledge. God is a scientist who has created an awesome universe with amazing complexity. He is the designer of infinitesimal atoms and molecules as well as huge galaxies. Man is enabled by knowledge and wisdom provided by God to explore his miraculous creation. The great scientist, Sir Isaac Newton, famously said of the cosmos: 'This most beautiful system of the sun, planets, and comets, could only proceed from the counsel and dominion of an intelligent Being. [...] This Being governs all things, not as the soul of the world, but as Lord over all; and on account of his dominion he is wont to be called "Lord God" *(Gk., pantokratr)*, or "Universal Ruler". [...] The Supreme God is a Being, eternal, infinite, [and] absolutely perfect.'[8] Our science lessons should evoke the awe and wonder of God and perhaps should end in worship of such a marvellous creator.

---

7 *1 Corinthians 12:27*

8 *Cited in Principia, Book III; Newton's Philosophy of Nature: Selections from his writings, p42, ed. H.S. Thayer, Hafner Library of Classics, NY, 1953*

English Language and Foreign Languages

Every language is important and reminds us of its origin at the tower of Babel in Genesis Chapter 11 when God frustrated the humanistic unity of mankind who were intent on self-aggrandisement and evil. Every language contains a structure and order in its grammar and a unique vocabulary, which, because language is spoken by the living, is always developing and changing. The learning of foreign languages is important to build relationships and cooperation. God is a communicating God who wants the gospel conveyed through language from the living to the living. How often a few words of a people's language spoken by a visitor open their hearts to that visitor and the message they carry! Learning language requires discipline and is not so attractive to a generation which has easy access through the internet in its various forms. We English joke that it is because we as a nation are so poor at learning languages that God has caused English to be the second language in so many countries all over the world! But that is a poor excuse!

Literature

Literature teaches us about relationships, motivations, choices and consequences. Literature is all about the power of story to engage the imagination and emotions, which Jesus used to great effect in his teaching. Literature also allows us to explore the characters of worthy heroes and the flaws of others so that we may learn vicariously about these issues and, hopefully, avoid making the same mistakes in our own lives. Literature teaches about worldview and can greatly add to our wisdom. We need to teach our pupils to discern the message inherent in each story.

Art

Art is often regarded by the undiscerning as a lesser subject. In many developing countries it is almost ignored and given little or no time on the timetable. Yet art is a demonstration of the fact that we are made in God's image; as he is creative in many different ways so we can be creative. All art is primarily based on the colour and design that God used to make our world. Sunrises and sunsets, birds, butterflies, flowers, land and seascapes, mountains all demonstrate the variety of an amazingly creative God. The world needs Christian artists and designers.

History

Although the glib saying: "History is His Story" may be too trite, yet it carries a truth. The Bible teaches that God is sovereign over the plans and affairs of mankind and the nations. As Daniel was shown in the Old Testament, God ordains seasons and the reigns of powerful cultures. Biblical history is linear not cyclical and proceeds towards the goal of the earth being *'filled with the knowledge of the glory of the Lord as the waters cover the sea'.*[9] In God's plan there is a beginning and an end to history on this planet. The beginning is depicted in Genesis and the end will be when Jesus returns. History reveals the way in which man's greed causes war and confusion yet ultimately God's purposes move steadily forward. The devotional promise, *"All things work together for good to those who love God and are called according to his purpose"*[10] is, in fact, an historical statement. The Bible states: *"Blessed is the*

---

9   Habakkuk 2:14

10 Romans 8:28

nation whose God is the Lord, the people he chose for his inheritance"[11] and "Righteousness exalts a nation."[12] Any nation which attempts to honour God and live by his standards will be blessed.

Geography

A Christian view of Geography reveals God the creator and designer of the physical world and the provider of resources for his people who dwell in it. It involves physical and demographic geography. A key biblical passage regarding the study of Geography (and also history) is found in the book of Acts: *'The God who made the world and everything in it is the Lord of heaven and earth and does not live in temples built by human hands. And he is not served by human hands, as if he needed anything. Rather, he himself gives everyone life and breath and everything else. From one man he made all the nations, that they should inhabit the whole earth; and he marked out their appointed times in history and the boundaries of their lands. God did this so that they would seek him and perhaps reach out for him and find him, though he is not far from any one of us.'*[13]

Today Geography has become a very wide-ranging subject incorporating many more concepts. The key concepts are: place, space, scale, interdependence, physical and human processes, environmental interaction and sustainable development, cultural understanding and diversity. However, modern geography now involves the study of how economies, societies and

---

11 Psalm 33:12
12 Proverbs 14:34
13 Acts 17:24-27

environments are interconnected. It builds on pupils' own experiences to investigate places at all scales, from the personal to the global. "Geography inspires pupils to become global citizens by exploring their own place in the world, their values and their responsibilities to other people, to the environment and to the sustainability of the planet."[14]

A Christian perspective explores these aspects in the light of God's creation and planning. One of the key biblical themes is stewardship of the planet God has given us; this includes how to develop the land responsibly and how to redress the negative effects of man's greed, exploitation and carelessness.

PE and Sport

This aspect of curriculum is a vital area for character training as well as skills. God created our bodies to be healthy and strong. He also wanted us to be responsible for stewarding and developing them. Physical exercise and pursuits are all part of stewarding our bodies and developing our strength, dexterity and skills. Athletics teaches the need for discipline in training, perseverance and pushing through physical challenges. The corporate aspect of team sports is also a key area of importance. Through these we learn how to cooperate, how to work as team, how to serve with our skill and how to aim to win but have grace when a better team excels over us!

---

14 National Curriculum: Geography Key stage 3, p2. www.qca.org.uk/curriculum

IT, Design and Technology:

Our society is a technological society. We need to be serving our pupils (who are often quicker than many of us!) in enhancing their skills but also in learning the right attitude to technology. In God's purposes Technology is to serve us both in accessing information and in administration, rather than ruling us. As one colleague put it: 'Go to the source of all information before going to your information source.' Design and Technology show us God the designer, the wise creator and efficient administrator; he created from nothing. He has made us in his image and gifted some specially to design and build or create from natural resources.

RE

The study of theology, through God's word, deserves a significant place and significant time on our timetable, apart from devotional times. In RE we are educating our pupils in the uniqueness of Christianity, including ethics and morality. It is also important for them to understand alternative worldviews so that they can appreciate where others of different beliefs are coming from and relate effectively to our multicultural society. We intend to prepare our pupils to be respectful of all other faiths and non-faiths from a secure foundational base in theology. We desire for them to relate effectively and compassionately to all people. The study of other main religions is important to equip them with this understanding.

From all these curricular aspects of knowledge, we can learn principles of wisdom and more of the fascinating nature of our God. God's aim is for us to apply our knowledge and use it to gain wisdom.

There are biblically based resources available for Christian educators.[15] There are also different models for the teacher to apply to curriculum.

One is the *'Creation, Fall, Redemption'* model which applies certain questions to each topic, as seen a lesson on the Water Cycle:

Creation: What was God's original intention for that object or process? Possible answer: water to cleanse, edify and refresh man.

Fall: The next question causes the pupil to ask: How did the Fall of mankind affect this? Possible answer: in the case of water: pollution through man.

Redemption: The question is: What might God want people to do to restore its original purpose and quality? The possible answer: to increase the availability of purer water by limiting and regulating industrial waste.

Another approach is the *'Way to Wisdom'* approach which uses principles of wisdom called 'heart concepts'. This approach can be applied to any government curriculum if need be. These are biblical truths which relate to the lesson topic which are biblically based and are to be at the heart of the lesson. An example would be that when teaching the Water Cycle we ask the question: What does this reveal about God or his creation? Our answer might be the following heart concept: 'The water cycle shows (or reveals) God's wise and economic provision'. (Ecclesiastes 1:7) A suitable biblical verse or

---

15 *One example: The series 'Bible Truth for School Subjects' by Ruth C. Haycock pub. The Association of Christian Schools International. See also 'Connecting Curriculum with Christ' by Mary Dunlop (available through HighLight).*

promise would be applied for the pupils to learn. e.g. *'And my God will meet all your needs according to his glorious riches in Christ Jesus.'*[16] [17]

Curriculum is obviously a huge area of education which needs revelation from God and persistent work by us. The Bible is not a text-book but it is a book of source revelations. Every Christian teacher is on a journey of discipleship into the revelation of how God's word shapes our knowledge and therefore our curriculum.

---

[16] Philippians 4:19

[17] This process is further explained and amplified in 'Diamonds Lost in the Sand' by the author, available on Amazon.

Chapter Six

CHARACTER EDUCATION

Education Is Not Just Information; It Is Transformation.

A popular world-wide view of education is that it is all about academic knowledge and ability. Progress in exams and the continual assessment and measurement is too often the only focus, bringing great pressure on pupils. However, kingdom education focuses not only on academic ability which is, of course, an important part of education, but also on the formation of character in our pupils. This reflects the heart of the Father. He said to the prophet Samuel who was asked to anoint a new king for Israel: *'The Lord does not look at the things man looks at. Man looks at the outward appearance, but the Lord looks upon the 'heart'*[1] The 'heart' refers to the character.

Character Education

'Character Education' has always been foundational and central to Christian schools — even if we didn't originally call it that!

As I said earlier, in forming a new Christian school back in the 1980s we did

---

1   1 Samuel 16:7

not know how to be a 'Christian' school. We learned by asking God how to do everything! We decided to put 'Character development' above 'Academics' and reflected this in our reports to parents by placing a summary of character at the head of the report before the academic results. The Christian school is a partnership with parents to make disciples of Jesus Christ by training character. In our parents' evenings we discussed the reports and decided how we were going to work together to help the pupil. Then we prayed together.

Components

- Valuing each pupil as uniquely created
- The Word of God—which is powerful to change the heart (Heb.4: 12)—sharp as a sword penetrating the heart
- Worship—where God's Spirit and the power of music and praise affects the character/personality (see chapter 7)
- Teachers as disciplers (mentors if you prefer) and role models aiming to live out following Christ
- The Holy Spirit—in the school, in the classroom, in the teacher, in the pupil

All of this begins in the Early Years/ Pre-school—these are vital foundations for acceptance, caring, nurturing and training in the love of God

God has created uniquely differing character/personalities. He loves variety. His original design is often corrupted by sin, the fall, or adverse parenting/even abuse or neglect. Each unique personality only finds its fulfilment through being restored to become more like Jesus.

Pupils need to be led to the challenge of being born again: *'Therefore, if anyone is in Christ, he is a new creation: the old has gone, the new has come.'*[2]

This begins the transformation of the personality/character but we are all in this process: *'We, who with unveiled faces all reflect the Lord's glory, are being transformed into his likeness with ever-increasing glory, which comes from the Lord, who is the Spirit.'*[3]

It is all the work of the Holy Spirit under God's direction. We teachers need to be working with this process — he wants to work through us. We provide unconditional acceptance and discipleship.

We are sowers of good seed — we do not often see the final results. Occasionally, we get the encouragement. Recently in India I met a young man called Yohan who told me that I last saw him in a small Christian school when he was three years old. He is now a fine Christian man of 30! He told me: "The values I was taught in the Christian school still guide me in life. They were a great foundation.' What an encouragement! The sowing was not in vain!

This extract from the poem *'Reflection'* by Oscar Romeo expresses it well:

> *This is what we are about*
> *We plant the seeds that one day will grow.*
> *We water seeds already planted,*
> *knowing that they hold future promise.*

---

[2] 2 Corinthians 5:17

[3] 2 Corinthians 3:17

> *We lay foundations that will yield future development*
> *We provide yeast that produces effects*
> *Far beyond our capabilities.*
>
> *We cannot do everything*
> *and there is a sense of liberation in realising that.*
> *This enables us to do something, and do it very well.*
> *It may be incomplete, a step along the way,*
> *an opportunity for the Lord's grace to enter and do the rest.*
>
> *We may never see the end results,*
> *But that is the difference*
> *between the master builder and the worker.*
> *We are workers, not master builders,*
> *Ministers, not messiahs.*
> *We are prophets of a future not our own.*

What we sow we shall reap.[4]

If we are sowing the word of God and his wisdom, it is good seed with the power in it to change hearts. Jesus said, *'Heaven and earth will pass away but my words will never pass away.'*[5]

---

4   Galatians 6:7-9

5   Matthew 24: 35

Character Education and the British Government

As Andrew Wilson from New Frontiers appropriately stated, 'Governments value what they want to measure but don't know how to measure what we value.' Character Education was finally given recognition under Prime Minister David Cameron. At the time of writing, our latest education minister, Damian Hinds, has said, 'Schools should aim for an ethos that develops pupils' character'. He specially emphasises resilience. As with all government education ministers all issues are tied to a successful economy. The ironic thing is that if integrity was being imparted all aspects of life would improve, including business and economy! Most employers are looking for workers of integrity.

Less Academic Pupils

We all know that pupils who are less academically able are often the ones who suffer in our state schools (and possibly in some Christian schools) because they are assessed as a person only on their academic performance. This leads to low self-esteem through constant failure and then to depression —possibly also anger and often results in anti-social or rebellious behaviour. This reaction is because they are not being recognised or valued as a person.

The Greek philosopher Aristotle got it right when he said, 'Educating the mind without educating the heart is no education at all.' Several decades ago, the famous Christian author, C.S Lewis, warned in his book, 'The Abolition of Man' that educators were in danger of producing people with brains but no chests. By 'chests' he meant hearts.

It is up to us as Christian educators to ensure that we restore this balance and recognise the valuable character qualities in every pupil.

The Phone and the i-World

This generation of pupils lives in an increasingly i-world where self reigns. Whilst not everything in America is reflected in the UK, yet research by an experienced American psychologist, Dr Jean Twenge, who has spent 25 years studying young people and has surveyed 11 million students, points out some interesting phenomena which we might do well to be aware of. She calls this generation the 'iGen generation.'[6]

She calls them 'super-connected kids growing up less rebellious, more tolerant, less happy and completely unprepared for adulthood.'

She believes a major factor is the smartphone and iphone. The youngsters she surveyed spent 6-8 hours a day of their leisure time on the phone or other digital media.

Results

Professor Twenge found that they were more protected but with less experience of being independent and making their own decisions. In addition, the phone has had the following effects:

---

6   *The following material is taken from the article 'TES Talks to Jean Twenge' in the Times Educational Supplement magazine. 9th March 2018*

- Adversely affects their ability to read books as they now read brief news and twitter feeds, preferring images rather than words.
- Crowding out the time they spend seeing friends in person. Even in school lunch breaks she found students complaining that they wanted to spend time with their friends but they were constantly on the phone.
- An obsession with safety
- Less interest in taking risks
- Less likely to drive; less likely to have a paying job or to date

In a global age, although this research was about the United States of America, it is likely to apply in varying ways to most countries where pupils have a mobile phone.

One way of helping pupils to develop good character qualities is to use stories and drama to illustrate different, desirable qualities as seen in famous people. These may be historical or living; fictional or non-fictional; they may be celebrities in athletics and sport or pioneers and explorers or we may choose those who are famous in our own culture's history. 'HighLight', an organisation aiming to promote desirable education has developed the following chart to illustrate these and provide a basis for character education.[7]

The character qualities also need to be considered in relation to curriculum as 'principles of wisdom'. The qualities and stories can be explored weekly through assemblies and tutor groups.

---

7   HighLight: registered charity no.1170549 www.highlightonline.org

DESIRABLE CHARACTER QUALITIES and ROLE MODELS

Several of the role models are repeated for different qualities. Wherever possible, heroes of a school's local community or culture should also be used. Note that JESUS CHRIST exemplifies every positive character quality as our role model.

1 MOTIVATION, DILIGENCE I am a person who is willing to work to achieve their aims and to inspire others	PAUL, NEHEMIAH	WILLIAM WILBERFORCE, DAME ANITA RODDICK, RICHARD BRANSON, WALT DISNEY, BILL GATES, STEPHEN SUTTON, QUEEN ELIZABETH II, ERIC LIDDELL, GANDALF
2. FOCUS, CONCENTRATION I have learned to concentrate and not be distracted	NEHEMIAH	DAVID BECKHAM, BILLY ELLIOT, STEPHEN SUTTON, PRINCE PHILIP, ALAN TURING, COUNT OF MONTE CRISTO
3. HUMILITY I am honest about my strengths and weaknesses	MOSES	CORRIE TEN BOOM, MAHATMA GHANDI
4. ATTENTIVE I actively listen	SAMUEL	THE SAMARITANS, ESTHER RANTZEN
5. RESPONSIVE, CONSCIENTIOUSNESS I aim to be thorough and to fulfil necessary requirements in my work	JOSHUA, NEHEMIAH, EZRA	QUEEN ELIZABETH II, MARTIN LUTHER KING GABRIEL OAKE (Thomas Hardy: Far from the Madding Crowd)

JESUS AS KING IN EDUCATION // 59

6. TEACHABLE I want to avoid arrogance and realise there is always more to learn and that education is a life-long process	PETER, DAVID, DANIEL	HELEN KELLER, JOHN MAXWELL
7. NEIGHBOURLINESS, CARE I care about others and look for opportunities to help where needed	GOOD SAMARITAN, DORCAS	MOTHER TERESA, DR BARNARDO, MARY SEACOLE (Jamaica), FLORENCE NIGHTINGALE, ALBERT SCHWEITZER, PRINCESS DIANA
8. CURIOSITY I like to discover more about this wonderful world and the people and wildlife in it.	SOLOMON	MADAME CURIE, NEIL ARMSTRONG, ISAAC NEWTON, MARCO POLO, CHRISTOPHER COLUMBUS, DAVID ATTENBOROUGH
9. COMMUNITY SPIRIT I realise that we are all part of a wider community and each one of us can make a positive difference	ESTHER	BISHOP DESMOND TUTU, ANGELINA JOLIE, DR BARNARDO, ABRAHAM LINCOLN, ELIZABETH FRY, MARTIN LUTHER KING
10. INTEGRITY I hold positive values and live by them	PETER, JOHN, JEREMIAH	JESUS CHRIST, ERIC LIDELL, QUEEN ELIZABETH II, RONALD REAGAN, ARAGORN
11. DIGNITY, INCLUSIVE I believe in the inherent dignity of other human beings	PSALMIST, Ps 139	NICK VUJICIC, MOTHER TERESA, DAVID LIVINGSTONE, ATTICUS FINCH

60 // JESUS AS KING IN EDUCATION

12. GENEROUS I share what I can	APOSTLES	BILL GATES, OPRAH WINFREY, BARONESS COX
13. TOLERANCE, RESPECT I respect others, their individual liberty, opinions and convictions as long as they are lawful within legal authority structures in their democratic societies	DANIEL	MAHATMA GANDHI, QUEEN ELIZABETH I, BISHOP DESMOND TUTU, WILLIAN WILBERFORCE, BARONESS COX, ANGELINA JOLIE
14. COURAGEOUS I will defend what is right	ABIGAIL, ESTHER, RAHAB, DANIEL, STEPHEN, DAVID, DEBORAH	MARTIN LUTHER KING, GRACE DARLING, ELLEN MACARTHUR, WILLIAM WILBERFORCE, ABRAHAM LINCOLN
15. PROBLEM-SOLVING I try to bring solutions	NEHEMIAH	STEPHEN HAWKING, WINSTON CHURCHILL, ALAN TURING
16. RELIABILITY, RESPONSIBILITY I want to be a person others can rely on to do what has been promised	RUTH, ABRAHAM, DANIEL	QUEEN ELIZABETH II, BILLY GRAHAM
17. TEAM-PLAYER I opt in to working with others under a leader	JOSHUA	DAVID BECKHAM, WAYNE ROONEY

18. GLOBALLY AWARE I am aware that I am part of a global community	PAUL	WILLIAM WILBERFORCE, WINSTON CHURCHILL
19. PATIENT I can wait when necessary.	ABRAHAM and SARAH	ANNE SULLIVAN (Helen Keller's teacher)
20. POSITIVE, OPTIMISM I am hopeful and positive, focusing on possibilities rather than obstacles and failures	JOSHUA, DANIEL, NEHEMIAH	NICK VUJICI, WALT DISNEY, MARTIN LUTHER KING, ANN OF GREEN GABLES, ATTICUS FINCH, BOB CRATCHIT
21. RESILIENCE, PERSEVERANCE and GRIT I will keep going and not give up, showing determination even through adversity	JOSEPH (OT), JOB, MOSES, DAVID, DEBORAH	WINSTON CHURCHILL, NELSON MANDELA, AMY JOHNSON, ABRAHAM LINCOLN, ELLIE SIMMONDS, ANDY MURRAY, DOUGLAS BADER, STEPHEN HAWKING, SCOTT of the ANTARCTIC, THOMAS EDISON, JIMMY VALVANO, MARTIN LUTHER KING, BILBO AND FRODO BAGGINS, GLADIATOR
22. HONESTY I aim to be truthful in my words and actions	PAUL, DAVID	JESUS CHRIST, MAHATMA GANDHI, GLADYS AYLWARD
23. LOYALTY I aim to maintain positive relationships even in hard times	RUTH, JONATHAN	PRINCE PHILIP, SAM GANGES (Lord of the Rings)

24. ADAPTABILITY I want to be flexible and ready to consider other possibilities and embrace necessary change	DAVID	RICHARD BRANSON, NICK VUJICIC, ELLEN MACARTHUR, SHERLOCK HOLMES
25. SERVING I am willing to serve others to help achieve positive objectives and/or their well-being. (This is not servility but the willingness to serve others, where appropriate.)	TIMOTHY	WILLIAM WILBERFORCE, MOTHER TERESA
26. A SENSE OF HUMOUR I can laugh at myself and others	JESUS	ADRIAN PLASS, PAM AYRES, SHREK
27. PERCEPTIVE I want to cultivate the ability to think consequentially and assess different situations appropriately	JOSEPH (OT)	ALBERT EINSTEIN, SIR ISAAC NEWTON, QUEEN ELIZABETH II
28. WISDOM I want to know how to best apply what I am and what I know	SOLOMON, ABIGAIL, DANIEL	KING SOLOMON, ASLAN

29. SELF-ACCEPTANCE, CONFIDENCE I am confident in who I am without arrogance	NEHEMIAH, PAUL, DAVID vs. Goliath, JOSHUA	SEB COE, GLADYS AYLWARD, DUCHESS OF CAMBRIDGE, BEAR GRYLLS, ELIZABETH BENNETT
30. CONSEQUENTIAL THINKING I consider the consequences of my choices and actions	DANIEL	ISAAC NEWTON, ALBERT EINSTEIN
31. CONSISTENCY, DRIVE and AMBITION I am willing to visualise targets and goals and work hard	NEHEMIAH, SOLOMON, JACOB	MALALA YOUSAFZAI, RICHARD BRANSON, NEIL ARMSTRONG, BILL GATES
32. SELF-CONTROL I know my boundaries and keep to them; I can say 'no' to myself	ABRAHAM	QUEEN ELIZABETH II, STEPHEN CURRY

We know that in every age God has wisdom available for us in the school communities we create as we seek first the kingdom of God in education. Above all, our relational approach to our pupils is the vital connection and will be the bridge over which learning and character development can take place.

Chapter Seven

THE POWER OF CHILDREN PRAISING THE KING'S PRESENCE

'From the lips of children and infants you have ordained praise because of your enemies to silence the foe and the avenger.'[1]

Praise and worship of God must be the central core of the school which is seeking the kingdom in education. Jesus makes special mention of the verse above on an occasion when he cleared the temple in Jerusalem of traders. The children had caught the spirit of who he was—possibly after hearing people praising him on his Palm Sunday journey into Jerusalem. They were shouting 'Hosanna to the Son of David'.

The chief priests and teaches of the law were indignant on hearing this praise. They asked, 'Do you hear what these children are saying?' Jesus replied referring them to the Psalms and quoting the verse above.

The praise of children is refreshing and usually energetic and full on! Children's faith is straightforward and fully trusting. More importantly, the effect

---

1   Psalm 8:2

of praise and worship is to turn them away from self-centredness to give thanks to their Creator. I used to ask our children in worship: 'Why do we praise God?' They answered 'Because he likes it!' In other words, we are pleasing him.

Praise as a Weapon Against Darkness

Yet there is another aspect which the last part of the verse expands further, saying that the praise of children has been 'ordained' or set in place by God '..because of your enemies, to silence the foe and the avenger.' This places a whole new dimension on praise. My NIV Bible footnote expresses it like this: 'The mighty God, whose glory is displayed across the face of the heavens, appoints (and evokes) the praise of little children to silence the dark powers arrayed against him.' Praise reaffirms the fact that these children were made in his image to reflect his glory through their praise. This praise coming from those so young demonstrates their simple faith and clearly seems to have a detrimental effect upon Satan, who is 'the foe' and 'avenger'. Praise can often be the weapon in difficulties, even as King Jehoshaphat, faced with huge enemy armies, sent out his choir ahead of his army and God gave him a tremendous victory without battle![2] Praise affirms faith, as also seen by the example of Paul and Silas imprisoned in chains and whipped after their preaching. This resulted in an earthquake, presumably sent by God, which released them and brought the jailer and his whole family to Christ![3]

---

2   NIV Study Bible, p776

3   Acts 16:12ff

Life in the River

One picture of life in God is the river of God. An experienced headteacher friend of mine, more experienced in the ways of the Spirit of God, encouraged me to keep inviting the Holy Spirit to keep flowing in the school.

The Christian school always faces the danger of becoming too set in its ways; religious legalism is one extreme and 'sloppy grace', where things become too loose and unrestrained is the other. How does a school stay fresh and relevant? I believe a huge part of the answer lies in 'staying in the river'.

What do we mean by 'the river'? The river is the life-flow, which comes from God. In Ezekiel 47 we read of this river of life which has its source in the Temple of Ezekiel's vision. The water flowed out of the Temple into the nation. As it flowed, Ezekiel discovered that it became deeper and wider — "a river that no-one could cross".[4] Ezekiel is told by the angel that this river makes even the Dead Sea fresh: "where the river flows everything will live".[5]

This image of the river of life, also found in Revelation, is a picture of the Holy Spirit who is the Spirit of love, life and wisdom who guides us into all truth.[6] It is good to remember that if, as we have emphasised, we are seeking first the kingdom of God in everything that we do, the Bible tells us that the kingdom of God is 'in the Spirit'.[7]

---

4   Ezekiel 47:5
5   Ezekiel 47:9
6   John 16:13
7   Romans 14:17

God came to us by his Spirit in many varied ways. Often in worship a supernatural peace would rest on the whole assembly—even boisterous young five and six-year-olds would be at rest. At other times he came in times of exuberant praise and there would be laughter and joy. One of our teachers was especially open to this and laughed a lot with the joy of the Lord, to the pupils' delight! At other times the children learned to exercise faith in the gifts of the Spirit from 1 Corinthians 12. The first time this happened was a surprise to us all. It was a few weeks after we had begun the school and children began to bring words of faith. We had a visiting educator who was totally astonished as he saw children aged 9-13 bringing words of knowledge for healing and praying for one another—especially as he didn't believe the gifts were for this present age!

Let the Children Come Unto Me

Our youngest infants learned in their other assembly times to praise God. Why? Because God likes it! Then, after praise, they would sit and wait quietly and practise listening to God. We were awed by the way God began to give them prophetic pictures and words. It began very simply. Even young children began to receive simple pictures from the Holy Spirit and have learned to ask what this means, just as Jeremiah was trained in simple prophecy by pictures God gave him of an almond branch and then a boiling pot.[8] He saw and then God gave the meaning.

Our children experienced the same process and began to grow in bringing a word from God and then asking him or a teacher to interpret what it meant.

---

8   Jeremiah 1:5 -14

We were amazed at some of the truths and revelations Father God was giving to his children. It seemed to us to reflect what the prophet Joel said so long ago about the future, *'Afterwards I will pour out my Spirit on all people. Sons and daughters will prophesy, your old men will dream dreams and your young men will see visions.'*[9] We experienced some of our children growing in this gift and bringing revelational words from God as teenagers; they also learned how to bring a word from the Bible.

Some of them in worship times even experienced direction from God about his future plans for them.

The Process

After waiting quietly, with their eyes closed, we would ask if anyone had seen anything or had any thoughts to share. In young children pictures began to be shared very simply. Often, they involved a good versus bad object—for instance, a decaying orange and a good one, or a flower in a vase of water and a dying one in an empty container. We would ask the children what they felt God might be showing them; very often they knew and would link these sorts of pictures to how God wanted us to receive his love, or his Spirit. Sometimes we interpreted. We found they had no barriers of unbelief like us! Of course, sometimes they copied another or made up something but, with encouragement, they grew in hearing God.

The most significant word came from a six-year-old-girl who saw a solid bar of pure gold and a flashing diamond. She said in explanation: "The diamond

---

9   Joel 2:28

was flashing and saying 'Look at me. Look at me' but it was Satan's trick. The Holy Spirit said: 'Look at the bar of gold which said nothing. The bar of gold is Jesus. He is pure gold.'" We were astounded. Another 6-year-old girl, brought us the following vision. She saw an ugly grey rock sticking out of the sea. "That's my life and its ugly", she said, without any prompting. Then she saw the rock sink under the sea. "The sea is God's love", she said, "and it's covering my life." The next scene was the rock reappearing on a gloriously beautiful island covered in flowers. "That's how Jesus has made my life beautiful", she said. With the help of a teaching assistant, Sarah painted the three scenes and I have shown them all over the world. Without fail, they impact audiences. Sarah had asked Jesus into her life a couple of weeks earlier and he brought a rather restless, frenetic girl into peace.

Changed Lives

Praise and worship on a regular basis bring the presence of God by his Spirit. It also changes and softens hearts and lives, reminding us of who we are and who God is, and that our lives are to be lived in service to him.

As we saw earlier, from Romans 14:17 the kingdom of God is 'in the spirit'. Nowhere is the Spirit more present than when we gather in worship. Worship brings the presence of the king and puts us in touch with the throne of God. Through prayer we have sometimes seen stubborn or unbelieving children change during worship. One teenager was so rebellious we were thinking we would have to expel him because of what he was doing in the school. We met with parents and, as a staff we prayed for several months; then, there were only days remaining until the end of term and his time in the school. On the last worship assembly God touched his heart and he totally changed. A couple of years later I had the experience of being led in worship at an adult meeting by this same boy!

On a less dramatic note, children experiencing fear or problems at home or at school have found more peace and help in these worship times. We have also, on some occasions, seen children with special needs greatly helped. In his presence is everything we need — and fulness of joy!

The promise expressed to the priest Eli in the Old Testament, was, *'Those who honour me I will honour.'*[10] This promise we can take and prove. As we honour God by giving time to worship him so he promises to honour us in the whole work of these children's lives, including their education.

Conclusion

God's promise, as we search for his Kingdom and listen to him, is that if we will make the kingdom will of God our priority, then all other things will be added to us. This is true for our schools and our whole education process. If we will put the King first and be dependent teachers who rely on God, his Word and his Spirit, he will lead us into all truth and bless our children's lives. According to his promise:

'All your sons (and daughters) will be taught by the Lord and great will be your children's peace' (Isaiah 54:13).

---

10 1 Samuel 2:30

www.ingramcontent.com/pod-product-compliance
Lightning Source LLC
Chambersburg PA
CBHW071254070526
44583CB00017B/2461